Journeys of Simplicity

—

Traveling Light

Journeys of Simplicity

—

Traveling Light

with

Thomas Merton

Bashō

Edward Abbey

Annie Dillard & Others

PHILIP HARNDEN

Walking Together, Finding the Way
SKYLIGHT PATHS Publishing
Woodstock, Vermont

Journeys of Simplicity:
Traveling Light with Thomas Merton, Bashō, Edward Abbey, Annie Dillard & Others

© 2003 by Philip Harnden

Page 108 constitutes a continuation of this copyright page.

Library of Congress Cataloging-in-Publication Data

Harnden, Philip.
Journeys of simplicity : traveling light with Thomas Merton, Bashō, Edward Abbey, Annie Dillard & others / Philip Harnden.
    p. cm.
Includes bibliographical references.
ISBN 1-893361-76-4 (HC)
1. Simplicity. I. Title.
BJ1496 .H35 2003
179'.9—dc21

                                    2002015992

10 9 8 7 6 5 4 3 2 1
Manufactured in Canada

SkyLight Paths Publishing is creating a place where people of different spiritual traditions come together for challenge and inspiration, a place where we can help each other understand the mystery that lies at the heart of our existence.
SkyLight Paths sees both believers and seekers as a community that increasingly transcends traditional boundaries of religion and denomination—people wanting to learn from each other, *walking together, finding the way*.

SkyLight Paths, "Walking Together, Finding the Way" and colophon are trademarks of LongHill Partners, Inc., registered in the U.S. Patent and Trademark Office.

Walking Together, Finding the Way
Published by SkyLight Paths Publishing
A Division of LongHill Partners, Inc.
Sunset Farm Offices, Route 4, P.O. Box 237
Woodstock, VT 05091
Tel: (802) 457-4000
Fax: (802) 457-4004
www.skylightpaths.com

To M. J.

Contents

I travel light; as light,

That is, as a man can travel who will
Still carry his body around because
Of its sentimental value.

—THOMAS MENDIP, THE VAGABOND SOLDIER
IN CHRISTOPHER FRY'S PLAY
THE LADY'S NOT FOR BURNING

I think over again my small adventures
my fears
those small ones that seemed so big

For all the vital things
I had to get and to reach

And yet there is only one great thing
the only thing

To live to see the great day that dawns
and the light that fills the world.

—OLD INUIT SONG

On Traveling Light

Twelve hundred years ago in China a middle-aged man named P'ang Yün loaded everything he owned onto a boat and sank it all in the Tung-t'ing Lake. After that, we are told, "he lived like a single leaf."

See him there in the early morning, treading water in the middle of the lake, watching the last bubbles rise from the depths. The air crisp and quiet. The lake misty and as still as sky. Then turning, stroking toward the shore.

Justine Dalencourt, a French Quaker, was forced to leave her home at Fontaine-Lavaganne when the German army invaded France in 1914. But first she planted her garden, saying, "I would rather they found something to eat at my house than that they should have to steal from others."

See her kneeling, covering the last seed. Patting down the moist soil. The warm spring sun. The full scent of the earth rising to her. The odd and distant thunder. Then standing, turning, walking away.

Traveling light—imagine this meaning: unencumbered journeying, a graceful way of traveling through life like a single leaf. Now imagine another: the light by which we journey, the light that shows the way. Our traveling light.

What would it mean to live like a single leaf? What would it mean to make one's life a journey of simplicity? a journey unencumbered, uncluttered, without distraction—a journey of focus and intention? a journey of lightness and light?

Quakers say a divine flame shines within each being. Every being. All beings. Would such a Light remind us that, after they steal our homes, the soldiers will be hungry? And to see that Deep Light—in ourselves, in others— must we first sink the boat?

In 1889, at age seventeen, my grandfather left family and friends in Sweden and sailed to America. He packed all his worldly goods in a small wooden chest. Today I have that chest near my writing desk. Its wooden slats weave around a rectangular frame; the hinged lid curves upward. The wood itself, now broken in places, has darkened.

Pondering this old chest, I see a young farm boy, fear and adventure in his eyes, setting aside all but the essential as he packs for his journey, summoning from within himself a quiet simplicity. I watch him board a boat in the early morning mist and launch into the deep.

I have not traveled much myself, but I do keep some handsome suitcases in my attic. Also two backpacks, three knapsacks, a duffel bag, a briefcase, several tote bags, a canvas rucksack, an ash-woven pack basket, three sleeping bags, and a tent or two. Looking at my grandfather's wooden chest, I realize it could not possibly hold everything I now require for a summer picnic. And unlike P'ang Yün, I cannot imagine where I would find a boat large enough to row all I own to the middle of some lake. Evidently, I intend to keep my worldly goods very much afloat.

Why? Do I lack the necessary lightness? the necessary Light?

For a number of years I have collected lists about traveling light. Most arose from journeys people have taken: place to place, day to day, birth to death. Each list simply describes what was carried, often in a rucksack, sometimes deeper within the traveler. I began collecting these lists, I suppose, because I found myself drawn to their spare poetry—a poetry of emptiness. I still do not fully understand why I find them compelling. Do I hear my grandfather's voice?

In the pages that follow, I have given each list a brief introduction. The lists themselves retain as much as possible the language, word order, and spelling of their sources. (The sources used for the lists, the introductions, and the quotations are given, in order of appearance, at the end of the book.)

I offer three suggestions to the reader.

First, approach these pages slowly and quietly, as you would a sleeping child. You could no doubt read them all in one night, but then you would lose your rest. So, instead, read a few pages at a time. They have stories to tell, questions to ask. Where do our journeys take us? What do we leave behind? What do we carry with us? How do we find our way?

Second, take these stories seriously but hold them lightly. Do not be disappointed or deceived. Remember that soldiers bent on massacre may sometimes travel as lightly as monks on pilgrimage. And pilgrims themselves may bear their own peculiar baggage, their own destructive schemes.

And third, ponder this mystery: We take delight in things; we take delight in being loosed from things. Between these two delights, we must dance our lives.

After sinking all his worldly goods, P'ang Yün devoted the rest of his life to his family, to Zen, to poetry, and to wandering.

Like a single leaf.

fewer the artifacts, less the words,
                    slowly the life of it
a knack for non-attachment.

—GARY SNYDER

Thomas Merton
(1915–1968)

French-born American Roman Catholic priest and Trappist monk

Father Louis, as Thomas Merton was known to his fellow monks, lived his last years as a hermit in the woods near his Cistercian abbey. His hermitage was small and unadorned, a cinder-block building with cement floors. He cut his own wood for the fireplace, hauled water from the abbey, cooked on a Coleman stove, and read by kerosene lamp. Eventually, as his health deteriorated, electricity was installed. Typically, he arose at 3:15 A.M. to begin the prayers of the day.

He was perhaps the first Trappist hermit of the modern era. He was surely a monk whose living and passing brimmed with irony. Vowed to silence, he was known around the world for his words. Cloistered with his brothers in Kentucky for twenty-seven years, he died half a world away in Bangkok, alone. An eloquent critic of the war in Southeast Asia, his body was flown home in the bay of a U.S. Air Force jet from Vietnam.

Among Thomas Merton's Personal Effects

Timex watch

one pair of dark glasses
   tortoise frames

two pairs of bifocal eyeglasses
   plastic frames

two Cistercian leather-bound breviaries

one rosary
   (broken)

one small icon on wood
   Virgin and Child

John Muir
(1838–1914)

Scottish-born American naturalist, inventor, writer, rover,
and crusader for wilderness preservation

John Muir was a lifelong pacifist who moved to Canada during the Civil War conscription. He was a mechanical wizard who refused to patent his inventions because "all improvements and inventions should be the property of the human race." When a factory accident temporarily blinded him, young Muir resolved to devote the rest of his life "to the study of the inventions of God." Upon regaining his sight, he set off alone on a thousand-mile botanizing walk from Indiana to the Gulf of Mexico.

"Only by going alone in silence, without baggage, can one truly get into the heart of the wilderness," he wrote. "All other travel is mere dust and hotels and baggage and chatter."

John Muir's Thousand-Mile Walk to the Gulf

In a rubberized bag
    comb
    brush
    towel
    soap
    change of underclothing

    copy of Burns's poems
    Milton's *Paradise Lost*
    Wood's *Botany*
    small New Testament
    journal
    map

a plant press

Henry Beston
(1888–1968)

American naturalist and writer best known for The Outermost House, *his chronicle of a solitary year on a Cape Cod beach*

"The world to-day," wrote Henry Beston, "is sick to its thin blood for lack of elemental things, for fire before the hands, for water welling from the earth, for air, for the dear earth itself underfoot."

To immerse himself in those elemental things, Beston had a neighbor build him a small house atop a dune on the farthest eastern reaches of Cape Cod, just thirty feet from the great Atlantic beach. His "outermost house" measured twenty feet by sixteen and contained two rooms (a bedroom and a kitchen/living room) with a brick fireplace in the wall between. Its only extravagance: ten windows, so Beston could see in every direction.

He came the first time to visit for a fortnight. But he lingered on for a year because, as he put it, "the beauty and mystery of this earth and outer sea so possessed and held me that I could not go."

Ten years after Beston's death a massive winter storm swept his house out to sea.

HENRY BESTON'S OUTERMOST HOUSE

Two oil lamps
    and various bottle candlesticks
    to read by

fireplace
    "crammed maw-full of driftwood"
    to keep warm

chest of drawers
    "painted an honest carriage blue"

table
wall bookcase
couch
two chairs
a rocker

a dish and crockery cupboard
two-burner oil stove
shelf
porcelain sink
water pump

knapsack
    for carrying in supplies

Ten windows
    "the four walls of the world"

11

Marcel Duchamp
(1887–1968)

French painter of the Dada movement

His wife, Teeny Matisse, once said she was struck by "how little space he took up."

MARCEL DUCHAMP ON WEEKEND TRIPS

Never a suitcase

two shirts
    worn one atop the other

a toothbrush
    in his jacket pocket

Annie Dillard
(b. 1945)

American writer, poet, and pilgrim

Dillard wrote the second half of her Pulitzer Prize–winning *Pilgrim at Tinker Creek* in a second-floor, cinder-block room with a window that overlooked a tar-and-gravel roof and a parking lot. "Appealing workplaces are to be avoided," she maintains. "One wants a room with no view, so imagination can meet memory in the dark."

In this writer's cell she kept her fielder's mitt (for afternoon softball games), some books, a bag of chocolate-covered peanuts, two or three quotes taped on index cards, a dozen different-colored pens, some piles of big index cards, and her messy yellow legal pads. One day she shut the window blinds and never opened them again.

More recently she set up shop in a tent in the yard of her Cape Cod house.

Annie Dillard's Writing Tent

Nine-by-twelve-foot canvas-roofed tent
    with sewn-in floor

tan coir rug
    fits precisely

desk
canvas chair
cot and mattress

heavy-duty extension cord
    powers computer on desk
    lamp by cot

red-patterned woven throws
    on cot

couple of blue dhurries

all sorts of clutter
    bird skeletons
    whalebones
    fishing floats
    stones

    dust them once a year

spiders and ants

Matsuo Bashō
(1644–1694)

Zen Buddhist wanderer and Japan's most revered poet

The poet took his pen name from a *bashō* (plantain) tree that grew in the garden of his little hut along the River Sumida. In 1684 he undertook the first of several journeys that he recorded in travel diaries of linked prose and verse. These were spiritual quests, not sightseeing trips, and perilous in every sense.

Bashō began his most celebrated journey in 1689 when he could no longer stay idle at home because, as he put it, the gods seemed to possess his soul. He patched his trousers, repaired his bamboo hat, bid farewell to his friends, and hoisted his pack onto his bony shoulders. Then he set out on the "narrow road to the deep north."

BASHŌ'S GREAT WALK

For cold nights
    a kimono of white paper
    treated with persimmon juice
    crumpled soft

a thin cotton kimono
a waterproof
writing materials
and so on

Farewell gifts from friends
could hardly leave them behind

    discomfort and vexation
    all the way

Edward Abbey
(1927–1989)

American author of Desert Solitaire, *ardent defender of the western wilderness, and all-around rascal*

On a June day, Abbey and his intrepid sidekick, one Ralph Newcomb, embarked on a float trip down the Colorado River. They wanted to see Glen Canyon before it was drowned behind a new dam.

Planning was not their forte. They forgot the life jackets (in their view, a pity). They forgot the rum (in their view, a tragedy).

Ed Abbey's Float Trip through Glen Canyon

Two rubber boats
   paddles

food supplies
   mostly bacon and beans
   for two weeks

Texaco road map of the state of Utah

wet bedroll
camping gear
   wrapped in a tarpaulin

rusty harmonica
pipe and tobacco

Father Zossima

Saintly Russian monk and elder of the monastery in Fyodor Dostoyevsky's novel The Brothers Karamazov

Tired and ill, Zossima rarely leaves his cell before he dies there. His bedroom, Dostoyevsky tells us, is "a little room furnished with the bare necessities." But the love and forbearance emanating from the old monk make this small room the moral still point in a world swirling with violence and corruption.

"Men have succeeded in accumulating a greater mass of objects," Zossima observes, "but the joy in the world has grown less."

FATHER ZOSSIMA'S MONASTERY BEDROOM

Narrow iron bedstead
    strip of felt for a mattress

candles

in the corner, under the ikons
    a reading desk
    a cross
    the Gospel

Dolores Garcia
(1889–198?)

One of the Old Ones of Spanish-speaking New Mexico,
devoted grandmother, and devout Roman Catholic

Psychiatrist Robert Coles moved to New Mexico in 1972
to continue his work with Spanish-speaking children. But
people kept telling him, If you want to know the children,
you must first know the Old Ones, *Una Anciana.*

He met Dolores Garcia when she was eighty-three.
She and her husband, Domingo, had always lived off the
land, with a garden, cows, and chickens. As they had for
fifty years, they still shared coffee and homemade bread
each breakfast, hard-boiled eggs each lunch. And always
her soup: When one pot emptied, she started another.

Of her seven children, only two sons survived. She
had taught her young ones that "we have our land, and
we feed ourselves and live the best lives we know how to,
and we must never feel empty and worthless . . . because
a salesman has beckoned us, and we have said No, I
haven't the money."

Mrs. Garcia Looks Around the Room

Made by her husband:
a round table
eight chairs
four more in the bedroom
the bureau there
the bed there
    a boughten mattress
    never a spring

Given by her sons:
Refrigerator
    mostly empty
    homemade butter and ice cream
    to give away
television
    to hold the family photos
    to watch the soaps
    with the sound turned off
clock in the bedroom
    they forget to wind
    except when son is coming

Her old friend:
the bread oven
    forty years
    every day

"My fingers would die
without the dough to work . . ."

Henry David Thoreau
(1817–1862)

American Transcendentalist, writer, and apostle of the simple life

We think of him as a writer at Walden Pond. But Thoreau's contemporaries knew him for his pencils. The improvements he introduced at his father's factory made the Thoreau pencil the finest of its time on this continent.

In 1857, Thoreau and a companion hired an Indian guide for a twelve-day canoe trip into the Maine woods. The man who preached "Simplify, simplify" assembled 166 pounds of baggage, enough to nearly swamp the canoe when they launched it.

But the cumbersome outfit he recommends for such a trip is most noteworthy for what it omits—the tool of both his trades: a pencil.

THOREAU'S OUTFIT FOR AN EXCURSION

Wear:
check shirt
stout old shoes
thick socks
neck ribbon
thick waistcoat
thick pants
old Kassuth hat

linen sack

Carry:
India-rubber knapsack
   with a large flap

two shirts (check)
one pair thick socks
one pair drawers
one flannel shirt
two pocket-handkerchiefs
a light India-rubber coat
   or a thick woolen one
two bosoms and collars
   to go and come with
one napkin
pins, needles, thread
one blanket, best gray
   seven feet long

tent, six by seven feet
    and four feet high in the middle
veil and gloves and insect-wash
    or better, mosquito-bars to cover all at night

best pocket-map
    and perhaps description of the route
compass
plant-book and red blotting-paper

paper and stamps

botany
small pocket spy-glass for birds
pocket microscope
tape-measure
insect-boxes

axe, full size, if possible
jackknife
fish-lines, two only apiece
    with a few hooks and corks ready
    and with pork for bait in a packet, rigged

matches
    (some also in a small vial
    in the waistcoat pocket)
soap, two pieces
large knife and iron spoon (for all)
three or four old newspapers

much twine
several rags for dishcloths
twenty feet of strong cord
four-quart tin pail for kettle
two tin dippers
three tin plates
a fry-pan

Provisions:
soft hardbread, twenty-eight pounds
pork, sixteen pounds
sugar, twelve pounds
one pound black tea
    or three pounds coffee

one box or a pint of salt
one quart Indian meal
    to fry fish in

six lemons
    good to correct the pork and warm water

perhaps two or three pounds of rice
    for variety

All into two large India-rubber bags
    water-tight and durable

Twenty-four dollars

The Other Henry Thoreau
(1817–1862)

American author, surveyor, and "self-appointed inspector of snowstorms"

After hammering together his ten-by-fifteen-foot cottage on Walden Pond, Thoreau declined the offer of a doormat because of the time it would cost him to shake it out. For a while he kept three limestone rocks on his desk. But he pitched them out the window in disgust when he found they required daily dusting. He kept but three chairs: "one for solitude, two for friendship, three for society."

Yes, he wasn't much of a carpenter; the site of his house was littered with bent nails. Yes, he lived there for only two years. Yes, his mother and sister did his laundry all the while. But try to forgive him. With his little house, Thoreau, more than anyone else, embedded in the American psyche an enduring vision of how we could live—if only.

THOREAU AT WALDEN POND

A bed
table
desk
three chairs

looking-glass
   three inches in diameter

pair of tongs and andirons
one kettle
a skillet
   and a frying-pan

dipper
wash-bowl
two knives and forks
three plates
one cup
one spoon

jug for oil
jug for molasses

one japanned lamp

Will Baker
(b. 1935)

American filmmaker, photographer, and writer

In 1979 Baker set out to meet the Asháninka, a native people living in a remote territory of central Peru. He had first read about them in an old *National Geographic*, found while rummaging through some dusty shelves in his barn. The photographs captivated him.

On the trail one day he paused to compare himself to the local travelers.

WILL BAKER ON THE TRAIL TO PUERTO OCOPA

Gringo gear:
sleeping bag
mosquito net
nylon cord
matches and candle
machete
Swiss army knife
extra pants, shirt, socks
cooking kit
camera, notebook
film, pens
dictionary and maps
toothpaste, brush
hairbrush, razor
soap, towel
poncho
first aid kit
raisin nut mix
tea
sombrero

Indian gear:
water bottle
machete

A Celtic Woman

Hebridean householder and keeper of the songs, prayers, and blessings of Celtic Christianity

Nineteenth century in the Outer Hebrides, those wild islands off the west coast of Scotland. A woman rises in the cold morning, her household still asleep. In her small hut—day in, day out—she begins the quiet, essential rhythms of daybreak: bathing her face, kindling the night-banked fire. With each act she breathes a prayer-of-three to the Trinity. Kneeling there on the earthen floor, she transforms her ordinary chores into sacrament, her daily journey into pilgrimage.

Esther de Waal, in her rich and sensitive writings on the Celtic way of prayer, so describes one anonymous woman of more than a hundred years ago.

On Pilgrimage with a Celtic Woman

Splashing my face
three palmfuls water

> God of Life
> Christ of Love
> Spirit of Peace

Triune of Grace

Kindling my fire
> thrice lift the peat

God, kindle in me
a flame of love

> to neighbor
> foe
> friend

my kindred all

Amen

Father Terence

Irish Catholic priest and Cistercian hermit on the coast of Australia in Bruce Chatwin's book The Songlines

About author Bruce Chatwin (1942–1989) it has been said, "He traveled light, and there was nothing—except friendship—he wasn't prepared to leave behind."

Chatwin describes Father Terence:

"He was a short man, with reddish hair, what was left of it, and not too many flaky brown teeth. He wrapped the teeth in a hesitant smile…

"He was working on a book of his own. It would be a 'manual of poverty.' He hadn't yet decided on a title.

"Today, he said, more than ever before, men had to learn to live without things. Things filled men with fear: the more things they had, the more they had to fear. Things had a way of riveting themselves on to the soul and then telling the soul what to do.

"He poured the tea into two red enamel mugs. It was dark and scalding. We sat a minute or two until he suddenly broke the silence: 'Isn't it wonderful? To live in this wonderful twentieth century? For the first time in history, you don't need to own a thing.'"

WHERE FATHER TERENCE LIVED

On the shores of the Timor Sea
on a dune of floury white sand

in a hermitage
    cobbled from corrugated sheet
    whitewashed
    walls guyed with cables against the wind

above the roof, a cross
    made from broken oar lashed together

black rubber flippers, snorkel, mask
swimming for hours along the reef
    with the shark

every evening at the typewriter
letters to friends all over the world
    a long correspondence
    with a Zen Buddhist monk
    in Japan

then, the lamp
reading into the night

seven years

Werner Herzog
(b. 1942)

German filmmaker whose unconventional work blends spirituality and nightmare, tenderness and epic dementia

Bruce Chatwin once called Werner Herzog "the only person with whom I could have a one-to-one conversation on what I would call the sacramental aspect of walking. He and I share a belief that walking is not simply therapeutic for oneself but is a poetic activity that can cure the world of its ills."

Near the beginning of Advent in 1974, Herzog received word that film critic Lotte Eisner, the guiding light of German cinema, lay dying in Paris. Herzog later wrote, "I said that this must not be, not at this time, German cinema could not do without her now, we would not permit her death. . . . I set off on the most direct route to Paris, in full faith, believing that she would stay alive if I came on foot."

In his hurry, Herzog left Munich without warm clothing or even a proper map. For twenty-one days of nearly constant rain and snow he slogged a compass course along dreary roadsides, through muddy fields. At night he slept in inns or barns or broke into weekend cottages. The pain of his blistered feet inside his new boots was soon overtaken by the pain of swollen tendons and ankles.

When he arrived at Eisner's bedside, he found her tired but recovering. She lived another nine years.

"I said to her, open the window, from these last days onward I can fly."

Herzog's Winter Walk from Munich to Paris

Boots, solid and new
compass
jacket
sweater and scarf
thin plastic poncho
duffel bag
    with the necessities

Acquired along the way
    storm cap
    long johns
    flashlight
    sticking-plaster, for blisters
    Shell Oil road map

Raymond Carver
(1938–1988)

Poet and short-story writer, often called America's Chekhov

The poet Tess Gallagher, Raymond Carver's friend and companion for eleven years, has described what she calls Carver's law. It was his practice, she tells us, "not to save up things for some longed-for future, but to use up the best that was in him each day and to trust that more would come."

At age fifty, Carver was told by his doctor that he would soon die from cancer. In one of his final poems, he asks himself if he has gotten what he wanted out of life. Yes, he answers, he has felt "beloved on the earth."

He continued to write and to plan, to hope. After Carver's death, Gallagher found an "errand list" in his shirt pocket.

RAYMOND CARVER'S ERRAND LIST

Eggs
peanut butter
hot choc

Australia?

Antarctica??

Sue

*Impoverished but skilled and gracious cook
in M. F. K. Fisher's 1942 book about wartime
food shortages,* How to Cook a Wolf

"She loved to eat," Fisher tells us, "and she apparently
loved, now and then, to eat with other people. Her sup-
pers were legendary."

She was seventy, alone, calm, not quite well. Her
house had the delicate dinginess of age and decay mixed
with the scent of bruised herbs. She spent less than fifty
dollars a year on food. Yet her salads and stews were
renowned because she blended them so skillfully, with
such thought and gratitude, and she cared enough to share
them with her friends.

At Sue's Table

In a little weatherbeaten house
on a big weatherbeaten cliff
    waves roaring at the foot
house seemed almost empty—
    no, stuffed with relics

a few plates
no knives
no electricity
only one candle
    whether two or eight at table
mysterious perfume of bruised herbs
    sage, gathered in the hills
    knew a hundred different kinds

wandering at night along cliff-tops and beaches
picking little shy weeds
    sea-spinach
    pink ice-plant
    fresh salt crispness
little bowls of chopped leaves
    fresh and cooked
common bowl of rice
    or potatoes, probably stolen
occasionally a fresh egg
    stolen, no doubt

one large Spode soup dish, full
    sliced cactus leaves
    lemon-berries
    dried crumbled kelp

tea, always

Ephraim M'Ikiara

Kenyan mountaineer and elder in the
Pentecostal Church of East Africa

Late one night in the 1980s, two British climbers,
bivouacked in the subzero cold atop Africa's second-highest
peak, were startled by the sudden appearance of a lone,
barefoot African man. He told them he had come to pray.

"At first it scared the hell out of us," the climbers
later told rangers. "Nobody climbs the mountain at night.
We had just spent a full day coming up the normal route
using ropes, ice axes, and pitons. Then this nice old man
arrives without even a pair of shoes."

Ephraim M'Ikiara stayed on Mount Kenya's 17,022-
foot Nelion summit for four days—praying, as he later
explained, for "the unification of all the religions of the
world." Meanwhile a rescue team was mobilized, con-
vinced no one could solo down the ice-covered pitches and
vertical overhangs. "Brother, can we show you the way?"
the rangers called out when they saw M'Ikiara descending.

"Was it you who showed me the way here?" he
replied, before disappearing into the mist and scrambling
down the mountain on his own.

Ephraim M'Ikiara Climbs Mount Kenya

In a battered leather bag
   huge Bible
   thin blanket
   piece of hemp rope
   small package of food
   kitchen knife to cut footholds in ice

a thin jacket

Barefoot

Japheth M. Ryder

Tenderhearted "dharma bum"—loosely
modeled after the poet Gary Snyder—
in Jack Kerouac's second-most-popular novel

"I admit it, I'm scared of all this American wealth, I'm just an old bhikku and I got nothin to do with all this high standard of living, goddammit, I've been a poor guy all my life and I can't get used to some things."

Japhy Ryder's Cabin near Corte Madera

Old clay jars
    exploding with picked flowers
straw mats on the floor
    no shoes
    no chairs
burlap on the walls
    prints of old Chinese silk paintings
    maps
    poems stuck on a nail
in the closet
    rucksack
    secondhand clothes

thin mattress
    Paisley shawl
    sleeping bag, rolled
books in orange crates
    Buddhist sutras
    Suzuki, haiku, poetry
woodstove

food stored on a shelf
    two onions
    an orange
    bag of wheat germ
    cans of curry powder
    rice
    dried Chinese seaweed
    bottle of soy sauce
    homemade brown bread

the simple monastic life

Emma "Grandma" Gatewood (1888–1973)

American hiker extraordinaire

She hiked the entire two-thousand-mile Appalachian Trail when she was sixty-seven years old. Then she hiked it again. Then she hiked it again. Always alone. Never with a sleeping bag, tent, backpack, map, or hiking boots—she preferred sneakers. She seldom cooked meals or built a campfire.

Grandma Gatewood had already raised eleven children when she read a magazine article about the Appalachian Trail. She resolved to be the first person to traverse it alone. She stood five-foot-two and on her first trip lost thirty pounds and wore out five pairs of sneakers.

Later, at age seventy-two, she walked the Oregon Trail to celebrate its centennial.

GRANDMA GATEWOOD ON THE APPALACHIAN TRAIL

In a homemade denim duffel bag
    sweater
    jacket
    scarf
    light wool blanket
        to sleep in
    plastic curtain
        for a tent
    two plastic eight-ounce baby bottles
        for water
    rain hat
    rain cape
        (doubled as ground cloth)
    flashlight
    Swiss army knife
    teaspoon
    tin cup
    matches
    Band-Aids and Mercurochrome
    safety pins, hair pins
    needle and thread, buttons
    soap and towel

simple foodstuffs
    bouillon cubes
    chipped beef
    raisins
    peanuts
    powdered milk
    salt

Ishmael

American sailor and narrator of Herman Melville's Moby-Dick

"Whenever I find myself growing grim about the mouth; whenever it is a damp, drizzly November in my soul; whenever I find myself involuntarily pausing before coffin warehouses, and bringing up the rear of every funeral I meet; and especially whenever my hypos get such an upper hand of me, that it requires a strong moral principle to prevent me from deliberately stepping into the street, and methodically knocking people's hats off—then, I account it high time to get to sea as soon as I can."

ISHMAEL GOES A-WHALING

Stuffed in an old carpet-bag
    a shirt or two

Fermina Daza

Colombian heroine of Love in the Time of Cholera, *Gabriel García Márquez's novel of the travails of life, love, old age, and death*

Somewhere along the Caribbean coast, in a place where the throes of love are sometimes mistaken for the symptoms of cholera, Florentino Ariza pursues Fermina Daza through fifty-one years, nine months, and four days of unrequited love. Only in her widowhood does Fermina Daza reluctantly acknowledge the overtures of this lifelong suitor. They embark on a river cruise together.

"It was the first time in half a century that they had been so close and had enough time to look at each other with some serenity, and they had seen each other for what they were: two old people, ambushed by death, who had nothing in common except the memory of an ephemeral past that was no longer theirs but belonged to two young people who had vanished and who could have been their grandchildren."

FERMINA DAZA'S RIVERBOAT TRIP

Eight days upriver
   five days back

only the bare necessities

half a dozen cotton dresses
toiletries

a pair of shoes
   for getting on and off the boat

house slippers

and nothing else

The dream of her life

Peter Matthiessen
(b. 1927)

American naturalist and novelist, cofounder of the Paris
Review, *sometime commercial fisherman and charterboat cap-
tain, and ordained Zen Buddhist monk*

Mourning the death of his wife, Peter Matthiessen set off
on a 250-mile trek across the high Himalaya. He headed
for Shey Gompa, a Buddhist monastery of the Kagyu sect,
perched on the Tibetan plateau. There he hoped to
glimpse the elusive snow leopard and to find the even
more elusive teacher that his soul was seeking.

PETER MATTHIESSEN ON CRYSTAL MOUNTAIN

A month of trekking

sausage
crackers
coffee
    all gone

sugar
chocolate
tinned cheese
peanut butter
sardines
  nearly finished

soon down to
    bitter rice
    coarse flour
    lentils
    onions
    a few potatoes, without butter

now the common miracles
    murmur of friends at evening
    clay fires of smudgy juniper
    coarse dull food

one thing at a time

John Jack
(ca. 1713–1773)

African enslaved as a cobbler by the shoemaker
Benjamin Barron of Concord, Massachusetts

When his master died, John Jack was made part of the estate, along with the livestock and furniture, that passed on to the widow. But slaves in New England could hire themselves out for wages when not at work for their masters. So through great labor and determination, John Jack earned enough to buy his own freedom by the time he was about forty-eight years old.

He built himself a cabin in the Great Meadows. He joined the church and paid taxes. His life insisted on its own dignity and would not be dissuaded, even by chains.

When he lay dying, at about age sixty, he bequeathed all he owned to Violet, an elderly slave of his late master's daughter.

John Jack's Bequest to Violet

Eight acres in the Great Fields
    and Great Meadows

a good pair of oxen
a cow and a calf

some farming tools

a Bible and psalm book

seven barrels of cider

Eric Hoffer
(1902–1983)

American migrant farmworker, gold prospector,
dishwasher, longshoreman, and self-educated "philosopher of
the docks," best known for his book The True Believer

Mysteriously blinded at age seven, Hoffer unexpectedly
regained his sight at age fifteen. Afraid the blindness would
return, he became a voracious reader to make up for the
schooling he had missed. As a migrant laborer in
California, he held library cards from practically every
library in the state—"my credit cards," he called them.

    "It has always seemed to me essential not to own
more than I can pack on my back."

Eric Hoffer on Clay Street, San Francisco

Second floor, one-room apartment
looked barely inhabited

bookcase on one wall
stuffed with haphazard assortment
    history, philosophy
    a few novels
    Montaigne, several editions

small table in the corner
    piled with notebooks
    a couple boxes of 3x5 cards

slightly larger worktable
student lamp

Webster's Unabridged on a stand

two straight wooden chairs
no rug, no easy chair, no phone
bed in the closet

no cooking, hated the smell
only boiled water for tea

thumbtacked to wall near door
unframed color print
    woman in antique dress
    (Pompeian wall painting)
    a gift

Bilbo Baggins

*Son of Bungo Baggins, grandson of the Old Took,
and diminutive hero of J. R. R. Tolkien's
mythological novel* The Hobbit

A hobbit hole means comfort, Tolkien tells us, and Bilbo
Baggins is a very comfortable hobbit indeed. His bed-
rooms, bathrooms, kitchens, and dining rooms have pan-
eled walls and carpeted floors. He has cellars and pantries
full of food and entire rooms devoted to clothes. To Bilbo,
"adventures" are nasty and uncomfortable affairs that make
you late for dinner.

But when he is visited by thirteen dwarfs and a wiz-
ard, "something Tookish" wakes inside him. Before he can
stop himself, he has left comfort behind to join one of the
great adventures of modern literature.

Bilbo Sets Off One Fine Morning

A borrowed dark-green hood
    (a little weather-stained)

a borrowed dark-green cloak
    (too large)

a lot of pocket-handkerchiefs

pipe
tobacco

Forgotten
    hat
    walking-stick
    money

Bill Wasovwich

Shy New Jersey backwoodsman and born-again Christian in John McPhee's book The Pine Barrens

McPhee met Bill Wasovwich in southern New Jersey's Pinelands, two thousand square miles of subtle beauty and emptiness virtually unknown to urban dwellers in the state. There Wasovwich made his living by working the woodlands' cycle: harvesting cranberries and blueberries, gathering sphagnum moss and pinecones in season. When not working, he went roaming in search of "events"— anything that caught his eye during a thirty-mile bush-whack through the woods.

Once Wasovwich came upon a jeep that the military had evidently dropped from the air and lost. He slowly disassembled it and packed it out piece by piece. At his cabin, he reassembled it. When he finally had the jeep back together, the army arrived and took it away.

BILL'S CABIN NEAR HOG WALLOW

Sturdy saltbox in the woods
   perhaps eighteen feet square
   clean within, almost empty

enameled cabinet
kerosene stove
small table
no bed or cot
   sleeping bag on the floor

Winchester rifle
   leaning against the doorjamb

on the table
   kerosene lamp
   strewn sheets of lined paper
     covered with writing
      Bible correspondence course
      Ambassador College

huge Bible
   bigger than an unabridged dictionary
   large print for reading by lamplight
   twenty-seven dollars

The Hermit of Tailaoshan

*One of several hundred Buddhist and Taoist
monks living the eremitic life in the mountains
of China, as related by Bill Porter in* Road to Heaven

In 1989 Bill Porter traveled to China to look for mountain
hermits. Although officials in Taiwan insisted that the
Communists had eradicated them all, Porter found otherwise.

One day on a mountain trail, a Buddhist layman led
him to the cave of an eighty-five-year-old monk. The
monk had moved to his cave-hermitage in 1939 after hav-
ing a dream in which the spirits of the mountain asked
him to become its protector. Villagers and disciples
brought him what little he needed. He had not come off
the mountain for fifty years.

After some conversation, the hermit asked Porter,
Who is this Chairman Mao you keep mentioning?

What the Hermit of Tailaoshan Needed

Not much

    flour
    cooking oil
    salt

once every five years or so
    a new blanket
    or set of robes

Jesus of Nazareth

*Jewish carpenter whose life and teachings inspire
the Christian faith*

"And what I say unto you, I say unto all: Watch."

JESUS SENDS FORTH THE TWELVE

Take nothing for your journey
save a staff

no knapsack
no bread
no money
not two coats

be shod with sandals

Go, preach
heaven is at hand

heal the sick
cleanse the lepers
raise the dead
cast out devils

George Washington Sears
(1821–1890)

*Pint-sized American shoemaker, writer, canoeist,
and self-described backwoods loafer*

When he began paddling Adirondack lakes and rivers, Sears, whose pen name was "Nessmuk," was entering his sixties and already suffering from the tuberculosis that would soon kill him. He stood five-foot-three and weighed 105 pounds. To manage the waterways alone, he had boat-builder J. Henry Rushton fashion him several ultralight cedar canoes. Sears explained that he wanted to find out how light a canoe it took to drown a man. The *Sairy Gamp*—a nine-foot beauty that weighed just 10½ pounds—wound up in the Smithsonian Institution.

His first trip, in 1880, lasted two months and covered five hundred miles. It was followed by similar cruises in 1881 and 1883. In failing health, sometimes too exhausted to portage or paddle, Sears was not above hitching a ride on another boat or accepting a hot meal at a guide's camp or enjoying an overnight at one of the many backwoods hotels of the day. But he never ceased to decry camping "with too much impedimenta, too much duffle."

"The temptation to buy this or that bit of indispensable camp-kit has been too strong, and we have gone to the blessed woods, handicapped with a load fit for a pack-mule. This is not how to do it. Go light; the lighter the better."

Nessmuk Cruises the Adirondacks

Rushton canoe
    less than eighteen pounds

double-bladed paddle

knapsack
    gum coat
    blanket
    pocket hatchet
    revolver

change of clothes
    blue woolen shirt
    pair of yarn socks

tent cloth
jackknife
fishing tackle

foraged old tomato can
    pot of hemlock tea

glorious campfire

a night just as a woodsman loves
    not a soul within miles
    owls in good voice
    a loon's strange wild cries
    through the night

William Least Heat Moon
(b. 1939)

*Native American (Siouan) traveler and writer with
de Tocqueville's eye and Thoreau's instincts*

Lost job. Lost marriage. Least Heat Moon chose to give
himself over to the circle. In a 1975 half-ton Ford
Econoline van, which he named *Ghost Dancing*, he set off
on a clockwise trip around the perimeter of the United
States. He stuck to the back roads, what the old gas station
maps showed as blue highways.

"If the circle had come full turn, I hadn't," he wrote
afterward. "I can't say, over the miles, that I had learned
what I had wanted to know because I hadn't known what I
wanted to know. But I *did* learn what I didn't know I
wanted to know."

Inside Least Heat Moon's Ghost Dancing

Sleeping bag and blanket
Coleman cooler
    empty but for a can of chopped liver
    given by a friend
    so there would always be something to eat
Rubbermaid basin and plastic gallon jug—
    the sink
Sears, Roebuck portable toilet
Optimus 8R white gas cook stove
    hardly bigger than a can of beans
knapsack of utensils
    a pot
    a skillet
U.S. Navy seabag of clothes
tool kit
satchel of notebooks, pens
    road atlas
    microcassette recorder
two Nikon F2 35mm cameras
    five lenses
two *vade mecums*
    Whitman's *Leaves of Grass*
    Neihardt's *Black Elk Speaks*
in billfold
    four gasoline credit cards
    $26

hidden under dashboard
    $428

on the dashboard
    a small gray spider, crawling

Arctic Tern *(Sterna paradisaea)*

Seabird of the gull family; migrates each year
between the Arctic and the Antarctic

During summer these birds nest in Greenland, Alaska, Canada, and islands of the Arctic. In autumn some migrate south along the Pacific coast of the Americas. Others fly east over the Atlantic, then south past Europe and Africa to the Antarctic Circle. In spring they retrace their route, for an annual round trip of more than 22,000 miles.

In 1970 an Arctic tern trapped alive in Maine had a leg band showing it to be thirty-four years old. In its lifetime it had probably flown some 750,000 miles, much of that over open seas. It weighed 4½ ounces. It was rebanded and released.

BAGGAGE FOR THE ARCTIC TERN'S 22,000-MILE MIGRATION

Frank O'Malley
(d. 1974)

*Legendary professor of English at the
University of Notre Dame*

He was a university professor who "never earned a doctorate, taught a graduate seminar, or wrote a book." He never married and, after entering Notre Dame as a freshman, never again lived outside a campus dormitory.

Yet O'Malley is widely esteemed as one of the great educators of our time. By all accounts, his lectures were inspiring and his devotion to his students unwavering. He knew them each by name and never forgot a one.

O'Malley disliked grades and once gave out more A's than he had students. Distribute the extras to others who need them, he told the dean.

Professor O'Malley's Dorm Room

All anyone could find in it:

a bed lumpy with books

old essays
  by students

old books
  by former students

old checks
  from students repaying loans

never cashed

Kamo no Chōmei
(1153–1216)

*Japanese Buddhist priest and hermit during
the early Kamakura period*

At age sixty, Kamo no Chōmei retreated to a mountain
called Toyama and built himself a little hut "for the last
leaves of my years." There, alone, he reflected on the many
calamities, both natural and political, that had ravaged
Japanese society at the end of the twelfth century.

He covered himself with clothes woven of wisteria
fibers and quilts of hempen cloth. He foraged the fields for
food and occasionally went begging in the capital city.

"My body is like a drifting cloud," he wrote in his
hut in the year 1212. "I ask for nothing, I want nothing.
My greatest joy is a quiet nap; my only desire for this life is
to see the beauties of the seasons."

The Hut on Toyama

Barely ten feet square
seven high

thatched roof
hinges on the joints of beams
    easy to move elsewhere

lean-to on south side
porch of bamboo
on the west, shelf for holy water
inside, on west wall
    image of Amida

on doors of reliquary
    pictures of Fugen and Fudō
on shelf above sliding door, facing north
three or four black leather baskets
    books of poetry
    music
    sacred writings
folding koto, lute

along east wall
    fern fronds and mats of straw: bed

nearby: square brazier
    burn brushwood
beneath window: desk

north of hut
    fenced garden
    many herbs

A "cocoon spun by an aged silkworm"

David and Goliath

The shepherd boy and the fearsome giant of
Hebrew scriptures

"Then said David to the Philistine, Thou comest to me
with a sword and with a spear and with a shield, but I
come to thee in the name of the LORD of hosts."

IN THE VALLEY OF ELAH

Goliath of Gath:
helmet of brass
coat of mail
    weighing five thousand shekels of brass
greaves of brass
    upon his legs
target of brass
    between his shoulders
spear's staff
    like a weaver's beam
spear's head
    weighing six hundred shekels of iron
shield bearer
    going before

David, son of Jesse:
staff in hand
sling
shepherd's bag
five smooth stones

Dorothy Day
(1897–1980)

American journalist, devout Roman Catholic, stalwart
pacifist, holy troublemaker, and cofounder
of the Catholic Worker movement

For fifty years she lived among America's urban poor, usu-
ally in one of the "houses of hospitality" that she and Peter
Maurin established to shelter and serve homeless people.
She distrusted government and its programs and believed
that Christians themselves should perform the works of
mercy: feed the hungry, clothe the naked, give drink to the
thirsty, visit the imprisoned, care for the sick, bury the
dead. Through her newspaper, her books, and her some-
times solitary witness, Dorothy Day "comforted the afflict-
ed and afflicted the comfortable."

DOROTHY DAY'S ROOM

Two flights up
bare of any luxury

simple furniture
   couple of chairs
   old wardrobe
   cot

next to the bed
   tiny statue of Joan of Arc
   wearing armor

manual typewriter

opera on the radio
   Wagner

shelf of well-thumbed books
the old favorites
   Bible
   Tolstoy, Dickens
   Desert Fathers
   Bernanos, Silone
   Dostoyevsky

Love in action
a harsh and dreadful thing
compared to love in dreams

Sir Ernest Henry Shackleton
(1874–1922)

British polar explorer

The year was 1915. The situation was this: Sir Ernest
Henry Shackleton and the twenty-seven members of his
Imperial Trans-Antarctic Expedition stood on the frozen
Weddell Sea and watched the ice pack slowly crush into
kindling their trapped ship, the *Endurance*. They were then
twelve hundred miles from any known human habitation.
They had seen no other human beings for nearly a year.
No one else knew they were in trouble or, for that matter,
where they were.

To survive, they were about to begin dragging their
two lifeboats on one-ton sledges across the ice pack.

Shackleton called all hands together. He told them
that each man would be allowed to bring only the clothes
on his back plus two pairs of boots, six pairs of socks, two
pairs of mittens, a sleeping bag, a pound of tobacco, and
two pounds of personal gear. Rid yourselves of every
unnecessary ounce, he advised.

For his own gear, he drew from under his parka the
Bible that Queen Alexandra had presented to them, with
her inscription on the flyleaf . . .

SHACKLETON'S WALK

Ripped from Queen Alexandra's Bible
    the flyleaf inscription
    the Twenty-third Psalm

    a page from the Book of Job:
        "Out of whose womb came the ice?
        And the hoary frost of Heaven
        Who hath gendered it?
        The waters are hid as with a stone
        And the face of the deep is frozen"

Laid the Bible in the snow

walked away

Robert Pirsig
(b. 1928)

American Zen Buddhist, metaphysician, professor of philosophy and rhetoric, and author of Zen and the Art of Motorcycle Maintenance

His famous book was conceived in 1968 after a long motorcycle trip with his twelve-year-old son, Chris, and two friends. They rode from Minneapolis across the Dakotas to the West Coast.

Robert had been in and out of mental hospitals for two years, and his son was on the verge of a breakdown during the trip. Chris eventually went to the San Francisco Zen Center and was recovering when he was killed by muggers in 1979.

Thirty years after his trip, Robert still has the motorcycle in his garage. But he no longer rides it.

ROBERT AND CHRIS PIRSIG'S MOTORCYCLE TRIP

Clothing:
two changes of underwear
long underwear
one change of shirt and pants each
one sweater and jacket each
unlined leather gloves
cycle boots
rain gear
helmet and sunshade, bubble
goggles

Personal Stuff:
combs
billfold
pocketknife
memoranda booklet, pen
cigarettes and matches
flashlight
soap in plastic container
toothbrushes and toothpaste
scissors
APCs for headaches
insect repellent
deodorant

sunburn lotion
Band-Aids
toilet paper
washcloth (in plastic box), towel

Books:
shop manual for cycle
Chilton's Motorcycle Troubleshooting Guide
Thoreau's *Walden*
 (read to Chris a sentence or two at a time)

Camping Equipment:
two sleeping bags
two ponchos and one ground cloth (converts to tent)
rope
USGS maps
machete
compass
canteen (couldn't find)
two Army-surplus mess kits
collapsible Sterno stove
some aluminum screw-top tins
 (for lard, salt, butter, flour, sugar)
Brillo
two aluminum-frame backpacks

Motorcycle Stuff:
standard tool kit under the seat
large adjustable open-end wrench
machinist's hammer

cold chisel
taper punch
pair of tire irons
tire-patching kit
bicycle pump
can of molybdenum disulfide spray
    (for the chain)
impact driver
point file
feeler gauge
test lamp

Spare Parts:
plugs
throttle
clutch and brake cables
points, fuses
headlight and taillight bulbs
chain-coupling link with keeper
cotter pins
baling wire
spare (used) chain

Peace Pilgrim
(1908–1981)

*Intrepid American walker and apostle
for world peace*

She was born Mildred Lisette Norman but gave up that name in 1953 when, as Peace Pilgrim, she embarked on the first of her seven cross-country pilgrimages for world peace. The previous year she had become the first woman to hike the entire Appalachian Trail. She began her new journey on the West Coast, passing out leaflets ahead of the Tournament of Roses parade in Pasadena.

For the next twenty-eight years, Peace Pilgrim walked "as a prayer" through every state, every Canadian province, and parts of Mexico. With a gentle persuasiveness, she urged upon anyone who would listen an unadorned message of nonviolence and disarmament. In 1964, having recorded 25,000 miles on foot, she stopped keeping track and began accepting occasional rides.

Peace Pilgrim neither carried nor accepted money and owned only what few things fit in the pockets of her tunic. "I walk until given shelter, fast until given food," she said.

In 1981 near Knox, Indiana, she died in a head-on collision while being driven to a speaking engagement.

THE WAY OF A PILGRIM

Navy blue long-sleeved shirt and slacks
running shorts and short-sleeved shirt
    (always ready for an invigorating swim)

navy blue socks
inexpensive blue sneakers
    one size too big ("so I can wiggle my toes")
    1,500 miles per pair

navy blue tunic with pockets all around
    on the front: PEACE PILGRIM
    on the back: 25,000 MILES ON FOOT FOR PEACE

in the tunic's pockets
    comb
    folding toothbrush
    ballpoint pen
    map
    leaflets
    correspondence

Nellie Bly
(1864–1922)

*American writer noted for her resourcefulness
as a world traveler and investigative journalist*

Nellie Bly was the pen name of Elizabeth Cochrane. As a
plucky young newspaper reporter, she once feigned insani-
ty to get inside a notorious asylum and expose its brutal
conditions to her readers. Other targets included sweat-
shops, jails, and corrupt politicians.

At age twenty-five, she proposed that her newspaper
send her on a race to circle the globe faster than Phineas
Fogg had traveled in Jules Verne's *Around the World in
Eighty Days*. Impossible, came her editor's reply. A woman
cannot safely travel alone. And besides that, a woman
would require too much baggage.

Seventy-two days, six hours, and eleven minutes later
she returned from her round-the-world journey, gripping
the small handbag that had been her solitary companion.

Around the World with Nellie Bly

The dress on her back
silk waterproof over her arm
£200 English gold in her pocket
Bank of England notes
    in a chamois-skin bag around her neck
some American gold and notes
    to test if known outside America

one ordinary hand-satchel
    passport no. 247
    two traveling caps
    three veils
    pair of slippers
    complete outfit of toilet articles
    ink-stand
    pens, pencils, and copy-paper
    pins, needles, and thread
    dressing gown
    last summer's silk bodice
    tennis blazer
    small flask and drinking cup
    several complete changes of underwear
    liberal supply of handkerchiefs
        and fresh ruchings

    jar of cold cream
        ("bulky and uncompromising . . . the bane of
        my existence")

Mohandas Karamchand Gandhi
(1869–1948)

*Great-souled ("Mahatma") father of independent
India, opponent of the caste system, and defender
of the rights of the so-called Untouchables*

At age sixty-two, on the eve of his 1932 fast to rid India of
Untouchability, Gandhi joked that he possessed few
clothes and fewer teeth.

THE MAHATMA'S EARTHLY POSSESSIONS

Two dinner bowls
a wooden fork and spoon

diary
prayer book
eyeglasses

three porcelain monkeys
    speak no evil
    hear no evil
    see no evil
    (gift from a Japanese Buddhist)

watch
spittoon
letter openers

two pairs of sandals

SOURCES

Epigraphs
Christopher Fry. *The Lady's Not for Burning: A Comedy*. New York: Oxford Univ. Press, 1949.

"Old Inuit Song." In *Never Cry Wolf*, a 1983 motion picture by Walt Disney Productions, based on the book by Farley Mowatt.

Gary Snyder. *Earth House Hold*. New York: New Directions, 1969.

On Traveling Light
P'ang Yün. *A Man of Zen: The Recorded Sayings of Layman P'ang*. Translated by Ruth Fuller Sasaki, Yoshitaka Iriya, and Dana Fraser. New York: Weatherhill, 1971, 1992.

London Yearly Meeting of the Religious Society of Friends. *Christian Faith and Practice in the Experience of the Society of Friends*. London: London Yearly Meeting of the Religious Society of Friends, 1960.

Thomas Merton
John Howard Griffin. *The Hermitage Journals*. New York: Andrews and McMeel, 1981; Garden City, N.Y.: Image Books, 1983.

———. *A Hidden Wholeness*. Boston: Houghton Mifflin, 1979.

John Muir
John Muir. *Thousand-Mile Walk to the Gulf*. Reprint. 1916. Dunwoody, Ga.: N. S. Berg,1969.

Thurman Wilkins. *John Muir: Apostle of Nature*. Norman: Univ. of Oklahoma Press, 1995.

Henry Beston

Henry Beston. *The Outermost House*. New York: Doubleday, 1928; New York: Henry Holt, 1949.

Marcel Duchamp

Calvin Tomkins. "Dada and Mama." *New Yorker*, 15 January 1996.

Annie Dillard

Annie Dillard. "Keeping It Simple." *Architectural Digest*, June 1996.

————. *The Writing Life*. New York: Harper and Row, 1989.

Matsuo Bashō

Matsuo Bashō. *The Narrow Road to the Deep North and Other Travel Sketches*. Translated by Nobuyuki Yuasa. Baltimore: Penguin Books, 1966.

————. *Narrow Road to the Interior*. Translated by Sam Hamill. Boston: Shambhala, 1991.

Albert Saijo. "Go-Light Backpacking." In *The Whole Hiker's Handbook*, edited by William Kemsley, Jr. New York: William Morrow, 1979.

Edward Abbey

Edward Abbey. *Desert Solitaire*. New York: McGraw-Hill, 1968; New York: Ballantine Books, 1971.

Father Zossima

Fyodor Dostoyevsky. *The Brothers Karamazov*. Translated by Constance Garnett. New York: New American Library, 1958.

Dolores Garcia

Robert Coles. *The Old Ones of New Mexico*. Albuquerque: Univ. of New Mexico Press, 1973.

Henry David Thoreau

Walter Harding. *The Days of Henry Thoreau*. New York: Alfred A. Knopf, 1965; New York: Dover Publications, 1982.

Henry David Thoreau. *The Variorum Walden and the Variorum Civil Disobedience*. Annotated by Walter Harding. New York: Washington Square Press, 1968.

———. *The Works of Henry D. Thoreau*. New York: Thomas Y. Crowell, 1940.

Will Baker

Will Baker. *Backward: An Essay on Indians, Time, and Photography*. Berkeley, Calif.: North Atlantic Books, 1983.

A Celtic Woman

Esther de Waal. *The Celtic Way of Prayer*. New York: Doubleday, 1997.

Father Terence

Bruce Chatwin. *The Songlines*. New York: Viking Penguin, 1987.

Michael Ignatieff. "On Bruce Chatwin." *New York Review of Books*, 2 March 1989.

Werner Herzog

Bruce Chatwin. *What Am I Doing Here*. New York: Viking Penguin, 1989.

Werner Herzog. *Of Walking in Ice*. London: Jonathan Cape, 1991.

Raymond Carver

Raymond Carver. *A New Path to the Waterfall: Poems*. New York: Atlantic Monthly Press, 1989.

Sue

M. F. K. Fisher. "How to Be Cheerful Though Starving." In *The Art of Eating*. New York: Collier Books, 1990. First published in *How to Cook a Wolf*. n.p., 1942.

Ephraim M'Ikiara

William Campbell. "The 'Impossible' Ascent: Shoeless on the Summit." *Mariah/Outside*, n.d.

Japheth M. Ryder

Jack Kerouac. *The Dharma Bums*. New York: Viking Press, 1958; New York: New American Library, 1959.

Emma "Grandma" Gatewood

James R. Hare. "Grandma Gatewood: A Legend Along the Appalachian Trail." In *Hiking the Appalachian Trail*, vol. 2, edited by James R. Hare. Emmaus, Pa.: Rodale Press, 1975.

Ishmael

Herman Melville. *Moby-Dick, or, The Whale*. Reprint. 1851. Evanston, Ill.: Northwestern Univ. Press, 1988.

Fermina Daza

Gabriel García Márquez. *Love in the Time of Cholera*. New York: Alfred A. Knopf, 1988; New York: Penguin Books, 1989.

Peter Matthiessen

Peter Matthiessen. *The Snow Leopard*. New York: Viking Press, 1978; New York: Bantam Books, 1979.

John Jack

Robert A. Gross. *The Minutemen and Their World*. New York: Hill and Wang, 1976.

Eric Hoffer

James T. Baker. *Eric Hoffer*. Boston: Twayne Publishers, 1982.
Calvin Tomkins. "The Creative Situation." *New Yorker*, 7 January 1967.

Bilbo Baggins
J. R. R. Tolkien. *The Hobbit.* New York: Ballantine Books, 1965.

Bill Wasovwich
John McPhee. *The Pine Barrens.* New York: Farrar, Strauss and
Giroux, 1968; New York: Ballantine Books, 1971.
———. "The Pine Barrens Revisited." *Living Wilderness,* Fall 1981.

The Hermit of Tailaoshan
Bill Porter. *Road to Heaven: Encounters with Chinese Hermits.* San
Francisco: Mercury House, 1993.

Jesus of Nazareth
Matthew 10; Mark 6; 13:37; Luke 9.

George Washington Sears
Christine Jerome. *An Adirondack Passage.* New York:
HarperCollins, 1994.
George Washington Sears. *The Adirondack Letters of George
Washington Sears, Whose Pen Name Was "Nessmuk."* Edited by
Dan Brenan. Blue Mountain Lake, N.Y.: The Adirondack
Museum, 1962.

William Least Heat Moon
William Least Heat Moon (William Trogdon). *Blue Highways: A
Journey into America.* Boston: Little, Brown, 1982.

Arctic Tern
John K. Terres. *The Audubon Society Encyclopedia of North
American Birds* (s.v. "Tern, Arctic" and "Migration"). New
York: Alfred A. Knopf, 1982.

Frank O'Malley
Kenneth L. Woodward. "The Life of a Great Teacher."
Newsweek, 21 October 1991.

Kamo no Chōmei

Kamo no Chōmei. "An Account of My Hut." In *Anthology of Japanese Literature*, edited by Donald Keene. New York: Grove Press, 1955.

David and Goliath

1 Samuel 17.

Dorothy Day

Robert Coles. *Dorothy Day: A Radical Devotion*. Reading, Mass.: Addison-Wesley, 1987.

Jim Forest. *Love Is the Measure*. Mahwah, N.J.: Paulist Press, 1986; Maryknoll, N.Y.: Orbis Books, 1994.

Studs Terkel. *Hard Times: An Oral History of the Great Depression*. New York: Pantheon Books, 1970.

Voices from the Catholic Worker. Edited by Rosalie Riegle Troester. Philadelphia: Temple Univ. Press, 1993.

Sir Ernest Henry Shackleton

Alfred Lansing. *Endurance: Shackleton's Incredible Voyage*. New York: McGraw-Hill, 1959.

Robert Pirsig

Stewart Brand. Review of *Zen and the Art of Motorcycle Maintenance*, by Robert Pirsig. *The Next Whole Earth Catalog*, edited by Stewart Brand. New York: Random House, 1980.

George Gent. "A Successful Pirsig Rethinks Life of Zen and Science." *New York Times*, 15 May 1974.

Robert Pirsig. *Zen and the Art of Motorcycle Maintenance*. New York: William Morrow, 1974. Also see the interview in the appendix of the twenty-fifth anniversary edition, 1999.

Peace Pilgrim

Peace Pilgrim. *Peace Pilgrim: Her Life and Work in Her Own Words.* Santa Fe, N.M.: Ocean Tree Books, 1991.

Peace Pilgrim website (www.peacepilgrim.com), maintained by Friends of Peace Pilgrim, Hemet, Calif.

Laurie Potteiger, Information Services Coordinator of the Appalachian Trail Conference, Harpers Ferry, W. Va. E-mail to author, 30 March 2001.

Nellie Bly

Susan Ware. "Girl Reporter Derring-Do." In *Modern American Women: A Documentary History*, edited by Susan Ware. New York: McGraw-Hill, 1997.

Mohandas Karamchand Gandhi

Dennis Dalton. *Mahatma Gandhi: Nonviolent Power in Action.* New York: Columbia Univ. Press, 1993.

Arun Gandhi, grandson of the Mahatma and director of the M. K. Gandhi Institute for Nonviolence, Memphis, Tenn. E-mail to author, 12 February 1999.

About the Author

Philip Harnden was the publisher of *The Other Side,* a magazine of spirituality and social action, for a dozen years. A Quaker, he has written on subjects as diverse as the land rights of Native Americans and the spiritual life of Fritz Eichenberg. A former correspondent for Religion News Service, Harnden has also been a commentator on North Country Public Radio. He lives in northern New York State, not far from the Canadian border.

About SKYLIGHT PATHS Publishing

SkyLight Paths Publishing is creating a place where people of different spiritual traditions come together for challenge and inspiration, a place where we can help each other understand the mystery that lies at the heart of our existence.

Through spirituality, our religious beliefs are increasingly becoming a part of our lives—rather than *apart* from our lives. While many of us may be more interested than ever in spiritual growth, we may be less firmly planted in traditional religion. Yet, we to want to deepen our relationship to the sacred, to learn from our own as well as from other faith traditions, and to practice in new ways.

SkyLight Paths sees both believers and seekers as a community that increasingly transcends traditional boundaries of religion and denomination—people wanting to learn from each other, *walking together, finding the way.*

We at SkyLight Paths take great care to produce beautiful books that present meaningful spiritual content in a form that reflects the art of making high quality books. Therefore, we want to acknowledge those who contributed to the production of this book.

PRODUCTION
Sara Dismukes, Tim Holtz,
Martha McKinney & Bridgett Taylor

EDITORIAL
Rebecca Castellano, Amanda Dupuis, Polly Short Mahoney,
Lauren Seidman, Maura D. Shaw & Emily Wichland

TEXT DESIGN & TYPESETTING
Dawn DeVries Sokol, Tempe, Arizona

JACKET DESIGN
Drena Fagen, New York, New York

JACKET/TEXT PRINTING & BINDING
Friesens Corporation, Manitoba, Canada

Other Interesting Books—
Spirituality

Lighting the Lamp of Wisdom: *A Week Inside an Ashram*
by *John Ittner;* Foreword by *Dr. David Frawley*

This insider's guide to Hindu spiritual life takes you into a typical week of retreat inside an ashram to demystify the ashram experience and show you what to expect from your own visit. Includes a discussion of worship services, meditation and yoga classes, chanting and music, work practice, and more.

6 x 9, 224 pp, b/w photographs, Quality PB, ISBN 1-893361-52-7 **$15.95**;
HC, ISBN 1-893361-37-3 **$24.95**

Waking Up: *A Week Inside a Zen Monastery*
by *Jack Maguire;* Foreword by *John Daido Loori, Roshi*

An essential guide to what it's like to spend a week inside a Zen Buddhist monastery.
6 x 9, 224 pp, b/w photographs, HC, ISBN 1-893361-13-6 **$21.95**

Making a Heart for God: *A Week Inside a Catholic Monastery*
by *Dianne Aprile;* Foreword by *Brother Patrick Hart,* ocso

This essential guide to experiencing life in a Catholic monastery takes you to the Abbey of Gethsemani—the Trappist monastery in Kentucky that was home to author Thomas Merton—to explore the details. "More balanced and informative than the popular *The Cloister Walk* by Kathleen Norris." —*Choice: Current Reviews for Academic Libraries*

6 x 9, 224 pp, b/w photographs, Quality PB, ISBN 1-893361-49-7 **$16.95**;
HC, ISBN 1-893361-14-4 **$21.95**

Come and Sit: *A Week Inside Meditation Centers*
by *Marcia Z. Nelson;* Foreword by *Wayne Teasdale*

The insider's guide to meditation in a variety of different spiritual traditions. Traveling through Buddhist, Hindu, Christian, Jewish, and Sufi traditions, this essential guide takes you to different meditation centers to meet the teachers and students and learn about the practices, demystifying the meditation experience.

6 x 9, 224 pp, b/w photographs, Quality PB, ISBN 1-893361-35-7 **$16.95**

Or phone, fax or mail to: **SKYLIGHT PATHS** Publishing
Sunset Farm Offices, Route 4 • P.O. Box 237 • Woodstock, Vermont 05091
Tel: (802) 457-4000   Fax: (802) 457-4004   www.skylightpaths.com
Credit card orders: (800) 962-4544 (8:30AM–5:30PM ET Monday–Friday)
Generous discounts on quantity orders. Satisfaction guaranteed. Prices subject to change.

Spiritual Practice

Finding Grace at the Center
The Beginning of Centering Prayer, 25th Anniversary Edition
by *M. Basil Pennington, OCSO, Thomas Keating, OCSO,* and *Thomas E. Clarke, SJ*

The book that helped launch the Centering Prayer "movement." Explains the prayer of *The Cloud of Unknowing,* posture and relaxation, the three simple rules of centering prayer, and how to cultivate centering prayer throughout all aspects of your life.
5 x 7¼, 112 pp, HC, ISBN 1-893361-69-1 **$14.95**

Three Gates to Meditation Practice
A Personal Journey into Sufism, Buddhism, and Judaism
by *David A. Cooper*

Shows us how practicing within more than one spiritual tradition can lead us to our true home.

Here are over fifteen years from the journey of "post-denominational rabbi" David A. Cooper, author of *God Is a Verb,* and his wife, Shoshana—years in which the Coopers explored a rich variety of practices, from chanting Sufi *dhikr* to Buddhist Vipassanā meditation, to the study of kabbalah and esoteric Judaism. Their experience demonstrates that the spiritual path is really completely within our reach, whoever we are, whatever we do—as long as we are willing to practice it.
5½ x 8½, 240 pp, Quality PB, ISBN 1-893361-22-5 **$16.95**

Praying with Our Hands: *Twenty-One Practices of Embodied Prayer from the World's Spiritual Traditions*
by *Jon M. Sweeney;* Photographs by *Jennifer J. Wilson;*
Foreword by *Mother Tessa Bielecki;* Afterword by *Taitetsu Unno, Ph.D.*

A spiritual guidebook for bringing prayer into our bodies.

This inspiring book of reflections and accompanying photographs shows us twenty-one simple ways of using our hands to speak to God, to enrich our devotion and ritual. All express the various approaches of the world's religious traditions to bringing the body into worship. Spiritual traditions represented include Anglican, Sufi, Zen, Roman Catholic, Yoga, Shaker, Hindu, Jewish, Pentecostal, Eastern Orthodox, and many others.
8 x 8, 96 pp, 22 duotone photographs, Quality PB, ISBN 1-893361-16-0 **$16.95**

Labyrinths from the Outside In
Walking to Spiritual Insight—a Beginner's Guide
by *Donna Schaper* and *Carole Ann Camp*

The user-friendly, interfaith guide to making and using labyrinths—for meditation, prayer, and celebration.

Labyrinth walking is a spiritual exercise *anyone* can do. This accessible guide unlocks the mysteries of the labyrinth for all of us, providing ideas for using the labyrinth walk for prayer, meditation, and celebrations to mark the most important moments in life. Includes instructions for making a labyrinth of your own and finding one in your area.
6 x 9, 208 pp, b/w illus. and photographs, Quality PB, ISBN 1-893361-18-7 **$16.95**

SkyLight Illuminations
Andrew Harvey, series editor

Offers today's spiritual seeker an enjoyable entry into the classic texts of the world's spiritual traditions. Each is presented in an accessible translation, with facing pages of guided commentary from experts, giving you the keys you need to understand the history, context, and meaning of the text. This series enables readers of all backgrounds to experience and understand classic spiritual texts directly, and to make them a part of their lives.

The Way of a Pilgrim: *Annotated & Explained*
Translation and annotation by *Gleb Pokrovsky*

This delightful account is the story of one man who sets out to learn the prayer of the heart—also known as the "Jesus prayer"—and how the practice transforms his existence. This edition guides you through the text with facing-page annotations explaining names, terms, and references. Illustrated.
5½ x 8½, 160 pp, Quality PB, ISBN 1-893361-31-4 **$14.95**

Bhagavad Gita: *Annotated & Explained*
Translation by *Shri Purohit Swami*; Annotation by *Kendra Crossen Burroughs*

"The very best Gita for first-time readers." —Ken Wilber

Millions of people turn daily to India's most beloved holy book, whose universal appeal has made it popular with non-Hindus and Hindus alike. This edition introduces readers to the characters; explains references and philosophical terms; shares the interpretations of famous spiritual leaders and scholars; and more.
5½ x 8½, 192 pp, Quality PB, ISBN 1-893361-28-4 **$16.95**

Dhammapada: *Annotated & Explained*
Translation by *Max Müller*; Annotation by *Jack Maguire*

The Dhammapada—words spoken by the Buddha himself over 2,500 years ago—is notoriously difficult to understand for the first-time reader. Now you can experience the Dhammapada with understanding even if you have no previous knowledge of Buddhism. Enlightening facing-page commentary explains all the names, terms and references, giving you deeper insight into the text. An excellent introduction to Buddhist life and practice. 5½ x 8½, 160 pp, Quality PB, ISBN 1-893361-42-X **$14.95**

Zohar: *Annotated & Explained*
Translation and annotation by *Daniel C. Matt*

The cornerstone text of Kabbalah, now with facing-page commentary that illuminates and explains the text for you.

The best-selling author of *The Essential Kabbalah* brings together in one place the most important teachings of the *Zohar*, the canonical text of Jewish mystical tradition. Guides readers step by step through the midrash, mystical fantasy and Hebrew scripture that make up the *Zohar*, explaining the inner meanings in facing-page commentary. Ideal for readers without any prior knowledge of Jewish mysticism.
5½ x 8½, 176 pp, Quality PB, ISBN 1-893361-51-9 **$15.95**

Religious Etiquette/Reference

How to Be a Perfect Stranger, 3rd Edition
The Essential Religious Etiquette Handbook
Edited by *Stuart M. Matlins* and *Arthur J. Magida*

The indispensable guidebook to help the well-meaning guest when visiting other people's religious ceremonies.

A straightforward guide to the rituals and celebrations of the major religions and denominations in the United States and Canada from the perspective of an interested guest of any other faith, based on information obtained from authorities of each religion. Belongs in every living room, library, and office.

COVERS:

African American Methodist Churches • Assemblies of God • Baha'i • Baptist • Buddhist • Christian Church (Disciples of Christ) • Christian Science (Church of Christ, Scientist) • Churches of Christ • Episcopalian and Anglican • Hindu • Islam • Jehovah's Witnesses • Jewish • Lutheran • Mennonite/Amish • Methodist • Mormon (Church of Jesus Christ of Latter-day Saints) • Native American/First Nations • Orthodox Churches • Pentecostal Church of God • Presbyterian • Quaker (Religious Society of Friends) • Reformed Church in America/Canada • Roman Catholic • Seventh-day Adventist • Sikh • Unitarian Universalist • United Church of Canada • United Church of Christ

6 x 9, 432 pp, Quality PB, ISBN 1-893361-67-5 **$19.95**

Also available:

The Perfect Stranger's Guide to Funerals and Grieving Practices
A Guide to Etiquette in Other People's Religious Ceremonies
Edited by *Stuart M. Matlins*
6 x 9, 240 pp, Quality PB, ISBN 1-893361-20-9 **$16.95**

The Perfect Stranger's Guide to Wedding Ceremonies
A Guide to Etiquette in Other People's Religious Ceremonies
Edited by *Stuart M. Matlins*
6 x 9, 208 pp, Quality PB, ISBN 1-893361-19-5 **$16.95**

Other Interesting Books—
Spirituality

God Within: *Our Spiritual Future—As Told by Today's New Adults*
Edited by *Jon M. Sweeney* and *the Editors at SkyLight Paths*

The future of spirituality in America lies in the vision of the women and men who are the children of the "baby boomer" generation—born into the post–New-Age world of the 1970s and 1980s. This book gives voice to their spiritual energy, and allows readers of all ages to share in their passionate quests for faith and belief. This thought-provoking collection of writings, poetry, and art showcases the voices that are defining the future of religion, faith, and belief as we know it.
6 x 9, 176 pp, Quality PB, ISBN 1-893361-15-2 **$14.95**

The Sacred Art of Listening
Forty Reflections for Cultivating a Spiritual Practice
by *Kay Lindahl;* Illustrations by *Amy Schnapper*

More than ever before, we need to embrace the skills and practice of listening. You will learn to: Speak clearly from your heart • Communicate with courage and compassion • Heighten your awareness for deep listening • Enhance your ability to listen to people with different belief systems.
8 x 8, 160 pp, Illus., Quality PB, ISBN 1-893361-44-6 **$16.95**

Spiritual Innovators: *Seventy-Five Extraordinary People Who Changed the World in the Past Century*
Edited by *Ira Rifkin* and *the Editors at SkyLight Paths;*
Foreword by *Dr. Robert Coles*

Dorothy Day, Black Elk, H. H. the Dalai Lama, Abraham Joshua Heschel, Krishnamurti, C. S. Lewis, Thomas Merton, Aimee Semple McPherson, Martin Luther King, Jr., Rabindranath Tagore, Simone Weil, and many more.

Profiles of the most important spiritual leaders of the past one hundred years. An invaluable reference of twentieth-century religion and an inspiring resource for spiritual challenge today. Authoritative list of seventy-five includes mystics and martyrs, intellectuals and charismatics from the East and West. For each, includes a brief biography, inspiring quotes and resources for more in-depth study.
6 x 9, 304 pp, b/w photographs, Quality PB, ISBN 1-893361-50-0 **$16.95**;
HC, ISBN 1-893361-43-8 **$24.95**

Or phone, fax or mail to: SKYLIGHT PATHS Publishing
Sunset Farm Offices, Route 4 • P.O. Box 237 • Woodstock, Vermont 05091
Tel: (802) 457-4000   Fax: (802) 457-4004   www.skylightpaths.com
Credit card orders: (800) 962-4544 (8:30AM–5:30PM ET Monday–Friday)
Generous discounts on quantity orders. Satisfaction guaranteed. Prices subject to change.

Spirituality

Releasing the Creative Spirit: *Unleash the Creativity in Your Life*
by *Dan Wakefield*

From the author of *How Do We Know When It's God?*— a practical guide to accessing creative power in every area of your life.

Explodes the myths associated with the creative process and shows how everyone can uncover and develop their natural ability to create. Drawing on religion, psychology, and the arts, Dan Wakefield teaches us that the key to creation of any kind is clarity—of body, mind, and spirit—and he provides practical exercises that each of us can do to access that centered quality that allows creativity to shine. "Will help you find the source of your own spiritual and creative powers." —*Yoga Journal*
7 x 10, 256 pp, Quality PB, ISBN 1-893361-36-5 **$16.95**

The Alphabet of Paradise: *An A–Z of Spirituality for Everyday Life*
by *Howard Cooper*

One of the most eloquent new voices in spirituality, Howard Cooper takes us on a journey of discovery—into ourselves and into the past—to find the signposts that can help us live more meaningful lives. In twenty-six engaging chapters—from A to Z—Cooper spiritually illuminates the subjects of daily life, using an ancient Jewish mystical method of interpretation that reveals both the literal and more allusive meanings of each. Topics include: Awe, Bodies, Creativity, Dreams, Emotions, Sports, and more.
6 x 9, 256 pp, Quality PB, ISBN 1-893361-80-2 **$16.95**

Winter: *A Spiritual Biography of the Season*
Edited by *Gary Schmidt* and *Susan M. Felch;* Illustrations by *Barry Moser*

Explore how the dormancy of winter can be a time of spiritual preparation and transformation.

In thirty stirring pieces, *Winter* delves into the varied feelings that winter conjures in us, calling up both the barrenness and the beauty of the natural world in wintertime. Includes selections by Will Campbell, Rachel Carson, Annie Dillard, Donald Hall, Ron Hansen, Jane Kenyon, Jamaica Kincaid, Barry Lopez, Kathleen Norris, John Updike, E. B. White, and many others. "This outstanding anthology features top-flight nature and spirituality writers on the fierce, inexorable season of winter.... Remarkably lively and warm, despite the icy subject." —★*Publishers Weekly* Starred Review
6 x 9, 288 pp, 6 b/w illus., HC, ISBN 1-893361-53-5 **$21.95**